A GIFT FOR:

_____

FROM:

_____

DATE:

_____

THE Thing i Like ABOUT YOU SWEETHEART

COUNTRYMAN®

A Division of Thomas Nelson Publishers
Since 1798

www.thomasnelson.com

The thing I like about my wife is that she saves me money every single day of the year!

Honey, you aren't going to believe what was on sale today!

The thing I like
about my husband
is that he's gifted
in the culinary arts.

The thing I like about you is that you almost always share the covers

(except on really cold nights, that is).

The thing I like about my husband is that he gets lots of exercise and stays in good shape.

The thing I like
about you, sweetheart,
is that you still
know how to get
my heart racing.

The thing I like
about my sweetheart
is that he still opens
the car door for me

(although he doesn't always
stick around to shut it anymore).

The thing I like
about you, sweetheart,
is that you know when
and how to be tough

(and I'm so glad we moved the big
screen down to the basement!).

19

The thing I like about my wife is that she depends on me for the manly tasks around the house.

The thing I like
about my sweetheart
is that he's faithful
and true, and he
has eyes only for me

(although I do help him avoid
temptation at the mall!).

23

The thing I like
about my husband
is that he shows
initiative—he believes
the early bird gets
the worm.

The thing I like about you is that you stay in shape and are incredibly disciplined in your fitness program.

The thing I like
about you, sweetheart,
is that you're a joy
to sleep with!

The thing I like
about you is
that you sing
such beautiful
love songs to me.

You are so beau-u-u-u-u-u-u-tiful, to me-e-e-e-e!

The thing I like about my wife is that she takes great care of herself and is up on all the latest beauty treatments.

The thing I like
about my husband
is that he's man
enough to express
his feelings.

35

The thing I like
about you is that you're
a world-class snuggler.

The thing I like
about my husband
is that he can whip
up a quick meal
that the kids seem
to love when
I'm not home
to help cook.

The thing I like
about my wife is
that she knows just
where to turn
when she needs
a listening ear
and a shoulder
to cry on.

The thing I like
about you is that you
know just what
to do when I'm
mad and fuming!

43

I don't care who made the cut.
We are going for a bicycle ride together!

The thing I like
about you, sweetheart,
is that you encourage
me in my love for
the great outdoors.

The thing I like
about my sweetheart
is that he is always
honest (and wise).

47

The thing I like about my wife is that she loves long, romantic, candlelit evenings with just me

(as long as they end by 10:00, of course!).

The thing I like
about you is your witty
sense of humor—
you still know how
to make me laugh!

The thing I like about you is that you know there's a time when you have to get tough with the kids.

The thing I like
about you, sweetheart,
is that you're still
a kid at heart!

The thing I like about my wife is that she has mastered the fine art of multi-tasking.

The thing I like
about my husband
is that he still
finds me attractive.

You want me to wear THAT on Valentine's Day?!

The thing I like
about my wife
is that she is full
of fresh and creative
ideas on decorating
and keeping the
house looking new.

The thing I like
about you is that
you're always ready
to help me with
hard work on hot,
sunny days in August.

The thing I like
about my husband
is that he can fix
just about anything
that's broken.

The thing I like
about my husband
is that he dresses
for success.

The thing I like about you is that you only want what's best for our family.

Yep, it's definitely broccoli casserole again.

The thing I like about my husband is that he's never lost his love for learning—he loves to spend time in his own special library.

The thing I like about my wife is that she is able to see beyond my faults.

"Honey, thanks for installing that new light fixture!"

The thing I like
about you, sweetheart,
is that you're so
easy to buy gifts for.

The thing I like about you is that you're always on time.

The thing I like about my husband is that he's the most patient man in the world when we shop.

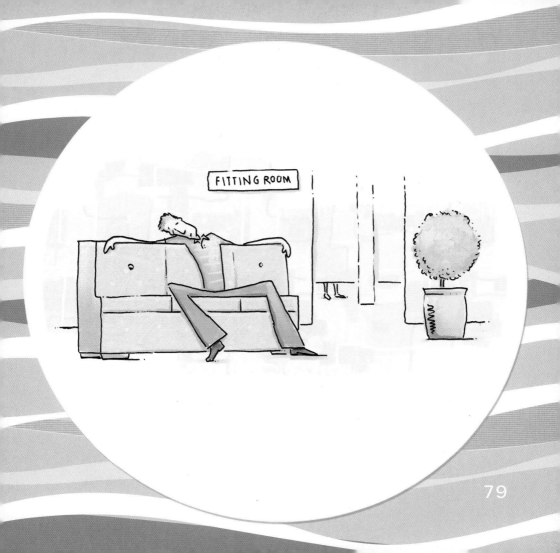

The thing I like
about my wife
is that she and I
love watching
the same kind
of videos together.

The thing I like
about you, sweetheart,
is that you have
those incredible
eyes that still
melt my heart.

The thing I like
about you is that
with you next to me,
I always look good!

The thing I like
about you, sweetheart,
is that you know how
to make a bad day
suddenly better.

The thing I like
about you is that
you have a wonderful
way of making up
after a fight.

The thing I like
about my husband
is that he makes me
feel safe and protected.

You wouldn't mind a back rub, would you?

The thing I like about my wife is that she knows how to cheer me up after a tough day!

The thing I like
about you, sweetheart,
is that you are one
unbelievable kisser

(and your hugs aren't too bad, either).

The thing I like about you is that you're all mine!

I thank my God every time
I remember you.

Philippians 1:3